Greenblatt Personal Firearms Record

Kim Greenblatt Publisher
Published In West Hills, California USA

Greenblatt Personal Firearms Record
by Kim Isaac Greenblatt

Disclosure: You should be aware of the laws and regulations at the Federal and state level where it concerns firearms and the collection of curios and relics. Be safe and do not handle firearms if you are tired, angry, under the influence of alcohol or drugs. Use common sense and take appropriate safety courses. If you find that you are having a problem, an addiction, or can't stop collecting, please seek professional help.

Published by Kim Greenblatt,
West Hills, California, United States of America.

ISBN-13 978-1-60622-007-8
May 2011

Dedicated to you, friend and collector. Please be safe, sane and happy with your collecting and try not to let your love of firearms be all consuming. Your family and friends want to see you once in awhile.

HOW TO USE THIS LOG BOOK:

Remember not to store the logbook with the firearms. In case a safe is stolen, you don't want your log stolen with it, did you? It doesn't hurt to have online back-ups or scans of your firearms but remember that you may not have electronic access if something really bad happens.

Please remember to be safe and smart. If you enjoy using this or any of my books, please tell your friends. Portions of every sale go to working for a cure for Rett Syndrome. Thanks!

NAME:

STREET ADDRESS:

CITY:

STATE:

ZIP CODE:

PHONE NUMBER:

INSURANCE COMPANY INFO:

Manufacturer	Model	Serial	Type	Caliber	Date	Cost	Purchase Location
Importer		Number	Action	Gauge	Acquired		Name and Address

Manufacturer	Model	Serial	Type	Caliber	Date	Cost	Purchase Location
Importer		Number	Action	Gauge	Acquired		Name and Address

Manufacturer	**Model**	**Serial**	**Type**	**Caliber**	**Date**	**Cost**	**Purchase Location**
Importer		**Number**	**Action**	**Gauge**	**Acquired**		**Name and Address**

Manufacturer	Model	Serial	Type	Caliber	Date	Cost	Purchase Location
Importer		Number	Action	Gauge	Acquired		Name and Address

Manufacturer	Model	Serial	Type	Caliber	Date	Cost	Purchase Location
Importer		Number	Action	Gauge	Acquired		Name and Address

Manufacturer	**Model**	**Serial**	**Type**	**Caliber**	**Date**	**Cost**	**Purchase Location**
Importer		**Number**	**Action**	**Gauge**	**Acquired**		**Name and Address**

Manufacturer	Model	Serial	Type	Caliber	Date	Cost	Purchase Location
Importer		Number	Action	Gauge	Acquired		Name and Address

Manufacturer	Model	Serial	Type	Caliber	Date	Cost	Purchase Location
Importer		Number	Action	Gauge	Acquired		Name and Address

Manufacturer	**Model**	**Serial**	**Type**	**Caliber**	**Date**	**Cost**	**Purchase Location**
Importer		**Number**	**Action**	**Gauge**	**Acquired**		**Name and Address**

Manufacturer	Model	Serial	Type	Caliber	Date	Cost	Purchase Location
Importer		Number	Action	Gauge	Acquired		Name and Address

Manufacturer	**Model**	**Serial**	**Type**	**Caliber**	**Date**	**Cost**	**Purchase Location**
Importer		**Number**	**Action**	**Gauge**	**Acquired**		**Name and Address**

Manufacturer	Model	Serial	Type	Caliber	Date	Cost	Purchase Location
Importer		Number	Action	Gauge	Acquired		Name and Address

Manufacturer	Model	Serial	Type	Caliber	Date	Cost	Purchase Location
Importer		Number	Action	Gauge	Acquired		Name and Address

Manufacturer	Model	Serial	Type	Caliber	Date	Cost	Purchase Location
Importer		Number	Action	Gauge	Acquired		Name and Address

Manufacturer	**Model**	**Serial**	**Type**	**Caliber**	**Date**	**Cost**	**Purchase Location**
Importer		**Number**	**Action**	**Gauge**	**Acquired**		**Name and Address**

Manufacturer	**Model**	**Serial**	**Type**	**Caliber**	**Date**	**Cost**	**Purchase Location**
Importer		**Number**	**Action**	**Gauge**	**Acquired**		**Name and Address**

Manufacturer	Model	Serial	Type	Caliber	Date	Cost	Purchase Location
Importer		Number	Action	Gauge	Acquired		Name and Address

Manufacturer	Model	Serial	Type	Caliber	Date	Cost	Purchase Location
Importer		Number	Action	Gauge	Acquired		Name and Address

Manufacturer	Model	Serial	Type	Caliber	Date	Cost	Purchase Location
Importer		Number	Action	Gauge	Acquired		Name and Address

Manufacturer	**Model**	**Serial**	**Type**	**Caliber**	**Date**	**Cost**	**Purchase Location**
Importer		**Number**	**Action**	**Gauge**	**Acquired**		**Name and Address**

Manufacturer	Model	Serial	Type	Caliber	Date	Cost	Purchase Location
Importer		Number	Action	Gauge	Acquired		Name and Address

Manufacturer	**Model**	**Serial**	**Type**	**Caliber**	**Date**	**Cost**	**Purchase Location**
Importer		**Number**	**Action**	**Gauge**	**Acquired**		**Name and Address**

Manufacturer	Model	Serial	Type	Caliber	Date	Cost	Purchase Location
Importer		Number	Action	Gauge	Acquired		Name and Address

Manufacturer	**Model**	**Serial**	**Type**	**Caliber**	**Date**	**Cost**	**Purchase Location**
Importer		**Number**	**Action**	**Gauge**	**Acquired**		**Name and Address**

Manufacturer	Model	Serial	Type	Caliber	Date	Cost	Purchase Location
Importer		Number	Action	Gauge	Acquired		Name and Address

Manufacturer	Model	Serial	Type	Caliber	Date	Cost	Purchase Location
Importer		Number	Action	Gauge	Acquired		Name and Address

Manufacturer	Model	Serial	Type	Caliber	Date	Cost	Purchase Location
Importer		Number	Action	Gauge	Acquired		Name and Address

Manufacturer	Model	Serial	Type	Caliber	Date	Cost	Purchase Location
Importer		Number	Action	Gauge	Acquired		Name and Address

Manufacturer	Model	Serial	Type	Caliber	Date	Cost	Purchase Location
Importer		Number	Action	Gauge	Acquired		Name and Address

Manufacturer	**Model**	**Serial**	**Type**	**Caliber**	**Date**	**Cost**	**Purchase Location**
Importer		**Number**	**Action**	**Gauge**	**Acquired**		**Name and Address**

Manufacturer	**Model**	**Serial**	**Type**	**Caliber**	**Date**	**Cost**	**Purchase Location**
Importer		**Number**	**Action**	**Gauge**	**Acquired**		**Name and Address**

Manufacturer	Model	Serial	Type	Caliber	Date	Cost	Purchase Location
Importer		**Number**	**Action**	**Gauge**	**Acquired**		**Name and Address**

Manufacturer	**Model**	**Serial**	**Type**	**Caliber**	**Date**	**Cost**	**Purchase Location**
Importer		**Number**	**Action**	**Gauge**	**Acquired**		**Name and Address**

Manufacturer	**Model**	**Serial**	**Type**	**Caliber**	**Date**	**Cost**	**Purchase Location**
Importer		**Number**	**Action**	**Gauge**	**Acquired**		**Name and Address**

Manufacturer	Model	Serial	Type	Caliber	Date	Cost	Purchase Location
Importer		Number	Action	Gauge	Acquired		Name and Address

Manufacturer	**Model**	**Serial**	**Type**	**Caliber**	**Date**	**Cost**	**Purchase Location**
Importer		**Number**	**Action**	**Gauge**	**Acquired**		**Name and Address**

Manufacturer	Model	Serial	Type	Caliber	Date	Cost	Purchase Location
Importer		Number	Action	Gauge	Acquired		Name and Address

Manufacturer	Model	Serial	Type	Caliber	Date	Cost	Purchase Location
Importer		Number	Action	Gauge	Acquired		Name and Address

Manufacturer	Model	Serial	Type	Caliber	Date	Cost	Purchase Location
Importer		Number	Action	Gauge	Acquired		Name and Address

Manufacturer	Model	Serial	Type	Caliber	Date	Cost	Purchase Location
Importer		Number	Action	Gauge	Acquired		Name and Address

Manufacturer	Model	Serial	Type	Caliber	Date	Cost	Purchase Location
Importer		Number	Action	Gauge	Acquired		Name and Address

Manufacturer	Model	Serial	Type	Caliber	Date	Cost	Purchase Location
Importer		Number	Action	Gauge	Acquired		Name and Address

Manufacturer	Model	Serial	Type	Caliber	Date	Cost	Purchase Location
Importer		Number	Action	Gauge	Acquired		Name and Address

Manufacturer	Model	Serial	Type	Caliber	Date	Cost	Purchase Location
Importer		Number	Action	Gauge	Acquired		Name and Address

Manufacturer	Model	Serial	Type	Caliber	Date	Cost	Purchase Location
Importer		Number	Action	Gauge	Acquired		Name and Address

Manufacturer	Model	Serial	Type	Caliber	Date	Cost	Purchase Location
Importer		Number	Action	Gauge	Acquired		Name and Address

Manufacturer	Model	Serial	Type	Caliber	Date	Cost	Purchase Location
Importer		Number	Action	Gauge	Acquired		Name and Address

Manufacturer	Model	Serial	Type	Caliber	Date	Cost	Purchase Location
Importer		Number	Action	Gauge	Acquired		Name and Address

Manufacturer	**Model**	**Serial**	**Type**	**Caliber**	**Date**	**Cost**	**Purchase Location**
Importer		**Number**	**Action**	**Gauge**	**Acquired**		**Name and Address**

Manufacturer	Model	Serial	Type	Caliber	Date	Cost	Purchase Location
Importer		Number	Action	Gauge	Acquired		Name and Address

Manufacturer	Model	Serial	Type	Caliber	Date	Cost	Purchase Location
Importer		Number	Action	Gauge	Acquired		Name and Address

Manufacturer	Model	Serial	Type	Caliber	Date	Cost	Purchase Location
Importer		**Number**	**Action**	**Gauge**	**Acquired**		**Name and Address**

Manufacturer	Model	Serial	Type	Caliber	Date	Cost	Purchase Location
Importer		Number	Action	Gauge	Acquired		Name and Address

Manufacturer	Model	Serial	Type	Caliber	Date	Cost	Purchase Location
Importer		Number	Action	Gauge	Acquired		Name and Address

Manufacturer	Model	Serial	Type	Caliber	Date	Cost	Purchase Location
Importer		Number	Action	Gauge	Acquired		Name and Address

Manufacturer	Model	Serial	Type	Caliber	Date	Cost	Purchase Location
Importer		Number	Action	Gauge	Acquired		Name and Address

Manufacturer	Model	Serial	Type	Caliber	Date	Cost	Purchase Location
Importer		Number	Action	Gauge	Acquired		Name and Address

Manufacturer	**Model**	**Serial**	**Type**	**Caliber**	**Date**	**Cost**	**Purchase Location**
Importer		**Number**	**Action**	**Gauge**	**Acquired**		**Name and Address**

Manufacturer	Model	Serial	Type	Caliber	Date	Cost	Purchase Location
Importer		Number	Action	Gauge	Acquired		Name and Address

Manufacturer	Model	Serial	Type	Caliber	Date	Cost	Purchase Location
Importer		Number	Action	Gauge	Acquired		Name and Address

Manufacturer	Model	Serial	Type	Caliber	Date	Cost	Purchase Location
Importer		Number	Action	Gauge	Acquired		Name and Address

Manufacturer	**Model**	**Serial**	**Type**	**Caliber**	**Date**	**Cost**	**Purchase Location**
Importer		**Number**	**Action**	**Gauge**	**Acquired**		**Name and Address**

Manufacturer	Model	Serial	Type	Caliber	Date	Cost	Purchase Location
Importer		Number	Action	Gauge	Acquired		Name and Address

Manufacturer	Model	Serial	Type	Caliber	Date	Cost	Purchase Location
Importer		Number	Action	Gauge	Acquired		Name and Address

Manufacturer	Model	Serial	Type	Caliber	Date	Cost	Purchase Location
Importer		Number	Action	Gauge	Acquired		Name and Address

Manufacturer	Model	Serial	Type	Caliber	Date	Cost	Purchase Location
Importer		Number	Action	Gauge	Acquired		Name and Address

Manufacturer	**Model**	**Serial**	**Type**	**Caliber**	**Date**	**Cost**	**Purchase Location**
Importer		**Number**	**Action**	**Gauge**	**Acquired**		**Name and Address**

Manufacturer	Model	Serial	Type	Caliber	Date	Cost	Purchase Location
Importer		Number	Action	Gauge	Acquired		Name and Address

Manufacturer	Model	Serial	Type	Caliber	Date	Cost	Purchase Location
Importer		Number	Action	Gauge	Acquired		Name and Address

Manufacturer	**Model**	**Serial**	**Type**	**Caliber**	**Date**	**Cost**	**Purchase Location**
Importer		**Number**	**Action**	**Gauge**	**Acquired**		**Name and Address**

Manufacturer	Model	Serial	Type	Caliber	Date	Cost	Purchase Location
Importer		Number	Action	Gauge	Acquired		Name and Address

Manufacturer	Model	Serial	Type	Caliber	Date	Cost	Purchase Location
Importer		Number	Action	Gauge	Acquired		Name and Address

Manufacturer	Model	Serial	Type	Caliber	Date	Cost	Purchase Location
Importer		Number	Action	Gauge	Acquired		Name and Address

Manufacturer	Model	Serial	Type	Caliber	Date	Cost	Purchase Location
Importer		Number	Action	Gauge	Acquired		Name and Address

Manufacturer	Model	Serial	Type	Caliber	Date	Cost	Purchase Location
Importer		Number	Action	Gauge	Acquired		Name and Address

Manufacturer	**Model**	**Serial**	**Type**	**Caliber**	**Date**	**Cost**	**Purchase Location**
Importer		**Number**	**Action**	**Gauge**	**Acquired**		**Name and Address**

Manufacturer	**Model**	**Serial**	**Type**	**Caliber**	**Date**	**Cost**	**Purchase Location**
Importer		**Number**	**Action**	**Gauge**	**Acquired**		**Name and Address**

Manufacturer	Model	Serial	Type	Caliber	Date	Cost	Purchase Location
Importer		Number	Action	Gauge	Acquired		Name and Address

Manufacturer	Model	Serial	Type	Caliber	Date	Cost	Purchase Location
Importer		Number	Action	Gauge	Acquired		Name and Address

Manufacturer	Model	Serial	Type	Caliber	Date	Cost	Purchase Location
Importer		Number	Action	Gauge	Acquired		Name and Address

Manufacturer	**Model**	**Serial**	**Type**	**Caliber**	**Date**	**Cost**	**Purchase Location**
Importer		**Number**	**Action**	**Gauge**	**Acquired**		**Name and Address**

Manufacturer	Model	Serial	Type	Caliber	Date	Cost	Purchase Location
Importer		Number	Action	Gauge	Acquired		Name and Address

Manufacturer	Model	Serial	Type	Caliber	Date	Cost	Purchase Location
Importer		Number	Action	Gauge	Acquired		Name and Address

Manufacturer	Model	Serial	Type	Caliber	Date	Cost	Purchase Location
Importer		Number	Action	Gauge	Acquired		Name and Address

Manufacturer	Model	Serial	Type	Caliber	Date	Cost	Purchase Location
Importer		Number	Action	Gauge	Acquired		Name and Address

Manufacturer	Model	Serial	Type	Caliber	Date	Cost	Purchase Location
Importer		Number	Action	Gauge	Acquired		Name and Address

Manufacturer	Model	Serial	Type	Caliber	Date	Cost	Purchase Location
Importer		Number	Action	Gauge	Acquired		Name and Address

Manufacturer	**Model**	**Serial**	**Type**	**Caliber**	**Date**	**Cost**	**Purchase Location**
Importer		**Number**	**Action**	**Gauge**	**Acquired**		**Name and Address**

Manufacturer	Model	Serial	Type	Caliber	Date	Cost	Purchase Location
Importer		Number	Action	Gauge	Acquired		Name and Address

Manufacturer	**Model**	**Serial**	**Type**	**Caliber**	**Date**	**Cost**	**Purchase Location**
Importer		**Number**	**Action**	**Gauge**	**Acquired**		**Name and Address**

Manufacturer	Model	Serial	Type	Caliber	Date	Cost	Purchase Location
Importer		Number	Action	Gauge	Acquired		Name and Address

Manufacturer	Model	Serial	Type	Caliber	Date	Cost	Purchase Location
Importer		Number	Action	Gauge	Acquired		Name and Address

Manufacturer	Model	Serial	Type	Caliber	Date	Cost	Purchase Location
Importer		Number	Action	Gauge	Acquired		Name and Address

Manufacturer	Model	Serial	Type	Caliber	Date	Cost	Purchase Location
Importer		Number	Action	Gauge	Acquired		Name and Address

Manufacturer	Model	Serial	Type	Caliber	Date	Cost	Purchase Location
Importer		Number	Action	Gauge	Acquired		Name and Address

Manufacturer	**Model**	**Serial**	**Type**	**Caliber**	**Date**	**Cost**	**Purchase Location**
Importer		**Number**	**Action**	**Gauge**	**Acquired**		**Name and Address**

www.ingramcontent.com/pod-product-compliance
Lightning Source LLC
Chambersburg PA
CBHW080038080426
R18101700001B/R181017PG42450CBX00002B/1
9781606220078